To Start You Painting

To my Wife

THERESA

*without whose interest, co-operation
and forbearance this book could
never have been written*

To Start You
PAINTING

AN INTRODUCTION TO LANDSCAPE
PAINTING IN WATER COLOURS

by F. C. Johnston

London
MACMILLAN & CO LTD
1963

MACMILLAN AND COMPANY LIMITED
St Martin's Street London WC2
also Bombay Calcutta Madras Melbourne

THE MACMILLAN COMPANY OF CANADA LIMITED
Toronto

ST MARTIN'S PRESS INC
New York

PHOTOTYPESET BY FILMSET LIMITED, CRAWLEY
PRINTED IN HOLLAND
BY VAN LEER & CO., AMSTERDAM

Foreword

SINCE PAINTING for pleasure has become so popular, a number of books have been published which inform the would-be painter that it is unnecessary to study or to undertake any basic training. All one has to do, it is suggested, is to have the urge and then 'have fun' with paint.

Exciting as this statement is, it is entirely misleading. Frustration would very soon follow any early fun. Real lasting joy in painting can only be achieved by thorough initial study: the groundwork.

To start you painting correctly and progressively I cannot think of a better guide than the author of this book. He has all the necessary experience in watercolour techniques, and the ability to impart his theory clearly and simply. Theories on how to paint are legion, but to be good, a theory must be based on experience, and proved through application and results.

Mr. Johnston is by profession an art teacher and painter, but what will interest the reader even more is that he has had long experience in helping the leisure-hour and holiday painter. He directs and teaches at a well-established summer school of painting, and it was there that he created and applied the method which is now embodied in this reliable and stimulating book.

I can confidently recommend 'To Start You Painting': it will do more than start you, it will *inspire* you.

EDWARD SWANN

Preface

F OR MANY YEARS I have been teaching Art to adults and to young people, not only in the classroom and studio, but also by taking parties on 'Painting Holidays'. I was impressed by their keenness, but what I found even more striking was the discovery of latent ability which had often been left to wither or remain undeveloped. I am now prepared to state that the vast majority of people have the ability to produce pictures, providing they have sympathetic teaching and genuine encouragement. Do not misunderstand me: I do not mean that they will become geniuses, but that they can produce work which will by no means disgrace them, and in some cases they may become painters of considerable talent and status.

It has also become evident during my years of teaching that most people, when they think of painting, think of landscape painting. Possibly our English tradition of fine landscape painters is the reason: a legacy of appreciation that has been inherited. Since the outdoor scene is also my own particular love, my circle of students has gradually grown. Several of them have now shown their work in the large London exhibitions. As the number of students has increased, so has my knowledge of their problems. Through trial and error, self-criticism, the help of fellow artists, the suggestions of the students, and many other influences I have slowly evolved the system described in this book.

This system has been developed for the real beginner, who is anxious to learn but rather timid of making the initial effort and uncertain where to begin. It is for just that kind of person that this book is intended, and if he or she can be shown the path that leads to creative landscape painting, I know that much pleasure will be theirs, and the writing of this book will have been justified.

F.C.J.

Contents

Figure 1a *and* b

I

First Essentials
and Simple Materials

I WANT YOU to imagine that two friends are walking along a towpath when they suddenly notice a scene which they both agree would make a fine subject for a picture. They sit down, make a sketch of it and show the results to us for our comments. The two sketches are reproduced in *Figure* 1.

The first thing we should have to praise these artists for is their ability to draw, for each has the scene nicely arranged on the paper and each has faithfully recorded what was there. So far, so good; but let us take our criticism a little further. The top drawing (a) is in 'line' only, and although the artist may have taken great care with it, the picture somehow fails to capture the real spirit of the riverside scene, with its lapping waters, its interesting shadows and its gently moving leaves. In other words, it lacks atmosphere. It does not have a feeling of space and distance. No doubt it could have been improved with 'shading' but even then such a strong outline would be very difficult to over-come.

Now let us look at the second drawing (b), which has been done with a small stick of charcoal. This I feel is very much better, as the scene now comes to life. Here we have a feeling of space and distance but, what is equally important, the various things which go to make up the scene have volume as well as shape —'form' is the word that artists use. This form has been obtained by carefully noting and placing the various lights and darks, and all the intermediate tones of grey. There are no outlines at all. The picture is made up of countless little patches of charcoal, each of its correct value of greyness, and when all are placed together we have a sketch that really captures the scene: the boat sits snugly into the bank, the tree casts its embracing shadows, and the distant hills give the impression that space separates them from the main subject of the picture.

A further interesting point is that the second picture looks very much like a black and white reproduction of a *painted picture*. Its effect is similar to that of a painting made with a brush, whereas in fact it has been produced mainly by smudging charcoal with a finger.

From this we can gather that charcoal drawing is an admirable prelude to painting, for not only will it make us observe our subjects in all their many tones, but it will also, by its paintable appearance, help us enormously when

I

later we start using colour. For this very good reason the painter-to-be is asked to make his first journey into the land of picture-making armed with a very powerful and expressive instrument—a humble stick of charcoal.

Now to make our first charcoal drawing (or, we could say, charcoal painting, for it will have a film of tone all over the paper, much the same as a film of paint), we need to know a little more about our materials. This is what we shall require:

1. Box of charcoal (willow)
2. Plastic rubber, for charcoal
   (sometimes known as putty rubber or kneaded rubber)
3. Fixative
4. Spray diffuser
5. Cartridge paper
6. Drawing board

These materials are not expensive and are easily obtainable. Cartridge paper is usually sold in sheets 22 in. by 30 in. and one sheet is sufficient for four studies. The drawing board can be a sheet of plywood, not too thick; 17 in. by 13 in. is a good size. Charcoal is made usually from vine or willow, and the willow type is quite suitable. The plastic rubber is used a small piece at a time, and moulded in the hand—a piece the size of a cherry is quite large enough. When it is being used, keep moulding it between finger and thumb and it will to a

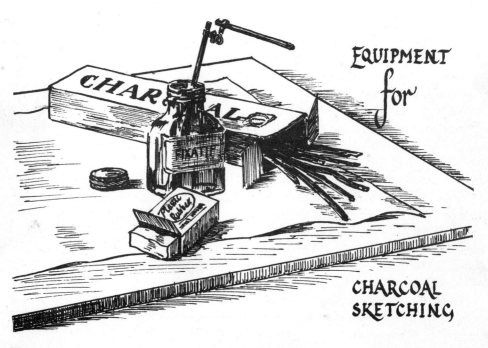

Figure 2

certain extent be self-cleansing. The fixative is really a very weak varnish and is applied to the finished picture to prevent smudging. It is sprayed on with the diffuser, which is used by placing the longer arm into the bottle, moving the arms to form a right-angle, and blowing down the shorter arm. Fixative is also available in aerosol containers.

With these materials, try a simple exercise which will accustom you to the feel of them. We are going to copy the tree study in *Figure 3*. Although we are copying, do not be afraid of a few personal touches, for in all painting the personal interpretation is to be encouraged, providing the essence of the scene is captured.

Rub down the end of the charcoal stick until you have a wide flat edge (inset), and with it make some broad even strokes across a piece of cartridge paper measuring about 7 in. by 9 in. Try to keep the strokes broad and even, and maintain the same pressure. Should the charcoal be at all scratchy, break off a small piece, make a fresh drawing edge, and continue with the broad strokes as in 'A'. The next step is to rub in the charcoal gently with a finger-tip until you have a pleasant even film of grey all over the paper. Should you find your finger-tips unco-operative, a little piece of cotton wool will help. Notice that the fur-like nature of the paper has given this film quite a pleasing texture, which would be destroyed if we rubbed too vigorously. This texture should always be preserved, for the paper is essentially one of our tools-of-the-trade and a good craftsman always knows the purpose and limitations of his tools; he never struggles and fights to make them perform something they are not meant to do.

The second stage 'B' is effected by the application of more charcoal and by careful rubbing, to make the tone darker at the top and gradually lighter to-wards the bottom. Finish this stage by putting in the darker area towards the bottom. This is done by simply increasing the pressure and thereby applying more charcoal. Blow on the sketch occasionally to dispose of any loose particles of charcoal which have not gripped the paper.

Now to use our plastic rubber. This is specially made to wipe out charcoal, and by moulding a small piece torn from the whole, lift out a streak or two with a bold firm stroke as in 'C'. Immediately we can see our sketch taking form—we have a bleached tree on a hill-top standing up proudly against the sky. True, it is rather like a ghost picture, for nothing yet is certain, but here we must exercise great caution and restraint. Surely the softness of the char-coal, the texture of the paper and the lack of any hard lines give the sketch a certain charm. Make no attempt at this or any future stage to over-dress the scene. Remember, softness and suggestion are the very nature of the materials we are using, and any attempt at fine detail would be impossible with our present materials. So 'draw' with your plastic rubber a few light passages as we have in 'C', not forgetting after each wipe to remould the rubber in your fingers.

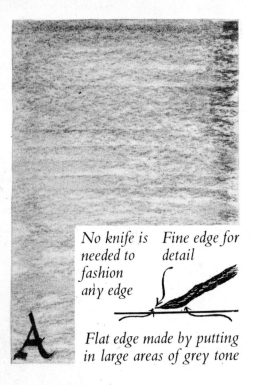

No knife is needed to fashion any edge

Fine edge for detail

Flat edge made by putting in large areas of grey tone

Figure 3. The four stages of making a charcoal sketch

In 'D' we have completed our sketch. We have assumed the source of light is from the left and above, and have therefore made the right-hand side the one in shadow. By putting in these extra darks where no sunlight could penetrate, and by lightening various sunlit areas, we have completed our sketch. We have attempted to show form by the effect of light and shade. Although this has merely been a warming-up exercise, it will give you, in black and white, all the necessary information to help you make a success of your painting later on. At all costs resist the temptation to draw blades of grass or separate leaves, but rather think always in terms of patches and masses of varying tones.

The next exercise involves a phenomenon which must be thoroughly understood if we are to make real progress. The atmosphere puts a veil of 'mist' between ourselves and the things we see. Therefore the further away an object is, the greater is the amount of 'mist' which our eyes are trying to penetrate. This makes distant objects very much more vague and quiet in tone than those which are near to us. The nearest things have well-defined highlights and shadows, but when we look further away the atmosphere plays its part, and the general effect is one of a gradual merging of lights and darks, until the far distance appears almost as one general tone, and the difference between the lighter and darker areas is very subtle indeed.

This effect can be likened to looking through a series of muslin curtains, such as stage designers use to show the 'faery glen' in the well-produced pantomime. The curtain is between the main characters and the scene behind, which looks quite far, far away. Immediately the lights go on, the filmy curtain is raised, and presto! the faery glen suddenly looks several yards nearer to us. In our sketch the very last thing we want to do is to lift this veil, for it is always there to some degree, and must be indicated if our landscape is to give any impression of depth, and feeling of distance.

By the same method of working as was used in the previous exercise, attempt the quick little sketch shown in *Figure* 4, which I have chosen from my sketch-book. It is a view taken from Salcombe in South Devon during the late evening. There is no detail whatsoever in this sketch and even the ruined castle is merely a suggestion. What is very important is the feeling that each range of hills recedes in succession, one behind the other. Not always is nature quite so kind in presenting a scene which so perfectly illustrates the point. May I now assume you have managed to copy it by the same method, that is, by coating the picture with a film of grey tone, then lifting out lights and putting in darks until you have it pretty much the same as the one printed here.

Assuming that you have managed to complete the sketch satisfactorily, you will notice that the tone of similar objects (in this case ranges of hills) gets considerably deeper as the distance between the observer and each object decreases. In other words, the nearer it is the deeper the tone. This can be observed even in the water and the sky, and by applying this knowledge we can create, on a flat surface, the illusion that the sky is dome-like and carries on over

Figure 4. To illustrate the changes in tone as the distance from the observer increases

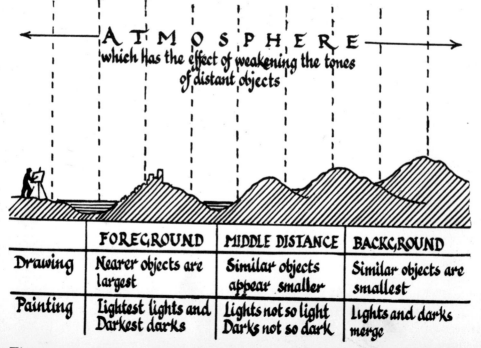

←— A T M O S P H E R E —→
which has the effect of weakening the tones
of distant objects

	FOREGROUND	MIDDLE DISTANCE	BACKGROUND
Drawing	Nearer objects are largest	Similar objects appear smaller	Similar objects are smallest
Painting	Lightest lights and Darkest darks	Lights not so light Darks not so dark	Lights and darks merge

Figure 5

our heads, and that the water is flat and gradually gets nearer until it laps at our feet. If you look out of the window at this moment (assuming it is daylight) you will immediately see the gradual deepening of tones as the sky passes overhead.

One further point that needs explanation is the handling of very light passages. Just as the darks get darker as objects get closer, so do lights appear to be lighter. Thus both the lights and darks on a *white* fence would be very much more pronounced on a fence that was close to us than they would be on one a little further away.

This phenomenon is even more clearly explained by *Figure* 5, which is a cross-section of our view of Salcombe, but please remember it is only a diagram.

These exercises, although interesting, are still only theoretical. Soon, however, we shall put them to the test out of doors. Fix the theory firmly in your mind, for it is not just a series of slick tricks to help you gain a cheap impression: it gives you the basis which you need to succeed with your painting. So often, when I have been out with sketching parties, have I seen students ignoring or forgetting this elementary fact, and they have tried loading the sketch with paint or charcoal—including more and more detail yet all the time becoming less and less happy with the result. It only needed a few minutes' work, softening the distance and sharpening the near-by portions to give the picture the effect which was becoming so elusive.

2

The Next Step:
Working out of Doors

MOST LANDSCAPE PAINTERS will tell you that whenever possible it is best to work direct from nature. In this country it is sometimes a little difficult, but the problems are well worth coping with. Our English climate gives us a light that is soft and pleasant, and the changes from one mood of weather to another are, once you are prepared to accept them, a constant source of beauty and delight.

Apart from the mackintosh and the extra woolly, a further piece of equipment that will be needed is a good lightweight stool. Take care when buying it, for an uncomfortable seat will cause cramp and a certain lack of dignity when eventually you try to stand up. Get one which has a reasonably large seat, has the absolute minimum of gadgets, and is not too low. You can now buy a good seat, made from an alloy, which is very strong and comfortable and is so light in weight that it can be carried on the little finger.

Another very useful item is a home-made viewfinder (*Figure 6*): This is merely a piece of card or plywood with a rectangular aperture cut in it, of the same proportions as the paper on which you work. It can be used rather like the press-photographer's viewfinder, and the solid margin will help you to isolate your subject as you look through the hole. By moving it close to your eye more can be seen; by moving it away less of the scene comes into view. Try it out first in the least likely places, and you will be surprised at the pictures you will discover, merely because the margin divorces your subject from all the confusing material that surrounds it. With this little aid I have often found subjects in the most surprising places: the heap of rubbish at the back of a farm, or the pattern of a few chimneys, to name only two.

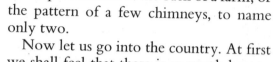

Now let us go into the country. At first we shall feel that there is so much beauty that we shall never be able to sort it all out. Therefore a little fore-thought will help: we must decide not to go for the vast panorama, but to look for things a little closer, and sometimes only a part of things. This is where our home-made

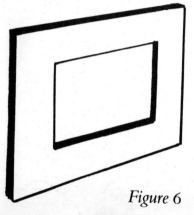

Figure 6

viewfinder will prove its worth, for now we shall not stagger on looking for the perfect subject; we might never have found it and might have had to return home with all our high hopes sadly shattered. Rather let us look at various parts of each scene by shifting and moving our viewfinder, and before long we shall see something and say to ourselves, 'Yes, I think I can manage that'.

Let us imagine that the photograph reproduced in *Figure 7* is a view of the general scene, and inside the black line is the part which, by the use of our viewfinder, has been selected as a suitable subject. This, then, is how I suggest you should proceed. First sit down comfortably for a few quiet thoughts on how to tackle the job in hand. Look at the scene not as so many leaves, so many walls and windows, and so many blades of grass, but rather in a general way, accepting *all* the scene *all* the time. By doing this you will very quickly see that you cannot accept the broad conception and at the same time itemise the scene with a lot of fidgety detail. The picture will gradually appear as a series of shapes of light, dark and intermediate tones. The ability to look at a subject in this broad way is very, very important. Often it is difficult, particularly if your temperament, or training in another craft or skill, has made your eye very susceptible to fine detail. Practice in this kind of observation is needed to understand the 'story' behind the picture, and this must be understood before any attempt at detail is made in the sketch. If you have not grasped the 'story', which is always one of the patterns made by the play of light, no amount of detail will help you. Having studied our scene, we now endeavour, by the use of charcoal, to retell its story.

Figure 7

Figure 8. Making a charcoal sketch from the actual scene

Figure 8. (cont.)

In this case, it is largely one of two flashes of light, one on the cottages and the other across the grassland. By smudging the paper with charcoal, leaving an irregular patch of light for the sky, we can then take our putty rubber and lift out the two all-important light passages, namely the meadow and the cottage wall, taking care to compare them in size and shape with our subject, and having due regard to their size in comparison with the size of the paper. Here again the viewfinder is of great help, for by looking through it you can see just how far up, down or across, these areas are situated, and it will also help to give a clearer idea of their comparative size. With these light passages established, you should have something like *Figure* 8A, and immediately you will notice that the story is beginning to unfold merely by these rather horizontal flashes of light. This was really the main feature that inspired us to transfer the scene to paper. The newcomer to painting must learn that the influence of light is of far greater importance than the introduction of slick pieces of detail which would probably merely destroy the effect of the lighting.

The next stage in the development of our study would be to compare what had been done so far with the actual scene, and to assess what was next in importance to help with the general interpretation. In this case it would be to give a feeling of flatness to the distant meadow, and also to show that the distant trees recede one behind another. Thus, we would darken the base of the trees where they and the meadow meet, and put a subtle light on the meadow at the same point (see *Figure* 8B). A few darker areas would then be put in to take the distant trees back a little. At this stage, too, we would insert a few of the more important dark passages in the eaves of the roof and in the foreground. At no time during these stages have we endeavoured to do any linear drawing, but have used our charcoal rather like paint, and have 'painted in' the various passages, not drawn them. Rember this important fact, as it is only in the final stages that line will be used, and then only if it is absolutely necessary, and helpful to our interpretation of the scene.

From what has been done so far, the beginner will see that painting is no hit or miss affair, where one pours one's material all over the paper with reckless abandon and little thought. Rather is the scene gradually built up from an understanding of essentials. The 'slosh and throw' method so often recommended is not truly helpful, and is liable to wreck any genuine progress.

Bearing this in mind, our sketch is now ready for its final touches. These we will put in as shown in *Figure* 8C. First, a subtle and gentle suggestion of foliage is made in the distant trees; not too crisp, for that would bring them too near. Next, let us put sufficient detail in our buildings, to give them a semblance of reality. This can be achieved by the inclusion of the extra shadow under the eaves and the dark rectangles to suggest doors and windows. If by now some of our lighter areas have become smudged, or need further attention, we shall rectify this as we proceed. Some of our foreground detail now needs attention, and the tall grasses on the right can be drawn in with the fine edge of the charcoal and a thinly shaped piece of rubber. The whole scene can then be studied and the final touches of light and dark included. It is only in this final stage that real drawing is used, and the inexperienced artist may find difficulty here because of a lack of drawing ability. This is quite understandable, and it may mean the need for extra drawing practice, but if the beginner can *see* mistakes and limitations at this point, he is obviously well on the way to becoming an artist.

Together, then, we have made our sketch—our first outdoor effort. Fix it with your fixative and date it, and as you do more and more studies refer back to it in order to measure your progress. Do not let your lack of experience worry you too much, for improvement will come. The main thing in the early stages is not to be too ambitious. Carefully choose subjects that do not present too many difficulties at once. Your viewfinder will help you with this. Always remember the materials with which you work, and consider how with them you can transfer your subject to paper. Consider its natural look; consider the obvious limitations of your medium. A good charcoal study should *look* like a charcoal study, and any attempt to make it look like a pencil drawing or an etching is asking both the material and yourself to achieve the impossible.

As you develop you will find that the strokes made with charcoal are very similar to those made with a brush, and by bearing this similarity to painting in mind, and by plenty of practice, the beginner will soon be ready to use

coal

a photograph merely as a short cut, allowing him to be permanently a fireside artist, the answer is a definite and resounding 'No!' If, on the other hand, a photograph is to be used mainly as a general reference, which means that something similar has been seen, and has been studied and thought about, then it could prove quite useful. If it is used, you must be extremely careful not to try for an exact copy. Your photograph is merely for reference, and your final piece of work should be an *interpretation*, not a copy. Furthermore, it must be sympathetic to the materials used, and have your own personal stamp upon it. If all this is borne in mind, then *use* your photograph. But remember, it is very much a second-best, and the finest place to work is always out of doors, in front of your subject.

Even when working on the spot the artist must be careful not to copy too much. That very fine artist and my good friend, Edward Swann, once remarked: '. . . never reduce the magnificent to a diagram'. The personal approach, allied to a sympathetic and thoughtful use of the materials, is so much more important than the minute rendering of detail. If the house you are painting has the feeling of shape; if you could walk into it and feel its protective shelter; if you can suggest the subtle mellowing effect of the weather —then you will have a building which will do far more for your picture than if you merely counted bricks. So off you go: good luck to you in your efforts —and may the weather be kind.

Figure 11. *Various charcoal techniques*

Figure 12

—*see page* 23

a, b. *Applying*
a wash

c.　*Using 'dry'*
colour gives an
unpleasant
effect

17

Figure 14. Charcoal and wash studies—see page 24

Figure 15 Simple exercises in wash—see page 27

3

Introducing Colour

THE PICTURE reproduced in *Figure* 13, page 18, depicts a scene in the old town of Hastings, and shows the large wooden sheds in which the fishermen dry their nets. The unusual shapes of these buildings, their interesting silhouette, and the contrasting modern lamp standard, made it a scene I felt I simply had to record. The method used was this: a charcoal drawing was made and thoroughly 'fixed', and water-colour paint was then floated over the whole thing in thin watery films of colour. These are called 'washes', and the complete process is known as 'charcoal and wash' painting. It is quite a well-known method of working. If desired, the order can be reversed by applying the colour first; but we will use the original method, as it is so obviously a good follow-on from our earlier work.

Paints are the next thing to consider, and although it is possible to buy various kinds of water-colour boxes already filled, I suggest you obtain an empty one and fill it yourself with pans of colour. The box I recommend is the type illustrated in *Figure* 16. This has a ring on the underside for your thumb, which will hold the box steady as you work, and has adequate wells or depressions in which the paint can be mixed. I suggest the following list of colours, for it has been for many years my basic palette and I have added to it only as general experience or some special circumstance has suggested. From it an adequate range of colours can be obtained.

Two yellows—Cadmium Yellow, Yellow Ochre
Two reds   —Alizarin Crimson, Vermilion
One blue   —Ultramarine Blue
One brown —Burnt Umber
One green   —Viridian
One grey   —Payne's Grey

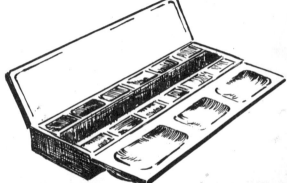

Figure 16

To Start You Painting

Here I feel I must insert a note of explanation. Nearly every professional artist I know has very definite ideas on what colours to use, and what to avoid. That, of course, is inevitable: otherwise we should find nothing delightfully personal about them or their work. The right choice is always one that is reached by experience, and by trial and error. I have suggested to you the foregoing palette because it is reasonably safe; and it is also one to which you can add as your study of this fascinating business of painting progresses. When buying your paints try if possible to purchase 'artist's' quality rather than student's; the extra expense will prove well worth it.

The same applies to brushes. You will need two, a No. 10 and a No. 7. Buy sables, if you can possibly afford them, for although expensive they are by far the best, and have a very long life. I have in my box a sable brush which is a great favourite, and is now nearly ten years old. Ox-ear hair brushes, which are not so pliable or hardwearing as sable, could be a first substitute. If some of this sounds a trifle expensive, remember that your materials are important and that in the long view good ones are usually cheaper . . . and there is always that very broad hint which can be dropped a few weeks before a birthday or Christmas!

The last requirement is a container for your water. I use a polythene cup, but any container which has a wide neck will do. A narrow vessel is unsatisfactory, as it will not allow sufficient space for the brush to be swirled around; and it is absolutely essential that you wash the brush after each application of colour. When working out of doors a flat bottle for your supply of water must be carried. Again, it is possible to get nice flat polythene ones, but usually students think up their own original ideas. A friend of mine hangs a rubber ball with a large hole in it from his paint-box, and for his reserve supply of water he carries a flat hot-water bottle. So far, in spite of many comments, he refuses to change, as he insists it is the easiest way of carrying this most necessary of materials.

Before getting down to work with our charcoal and wash study, one extra bit of preparation is needed. It concerns the paper. As you know, if water is dropped on to paper it will, unless the paper is very stout, make it wrinkle and buckle. This has to be avoided, as otherwise our paint would run into little pools and rivers and completely destroy the effect we desire. To overcome the difficulty we stretch and secure the paper to the board, and this is done as follows:

First sponge the paper on both sides so that it is uniformly wet. Now place it in the centre of your board and as flat as you can. Sponge off any surplus water and then with a strip of one-inch gummed paper (not Sellotape) stick down one of the long edges, keeping half the width of the gummed paper on the drawing-board and the other half on the cartridge paper. Again smooth your paper and secure next the other long edge and finally the two short ones. Do not be worried if there are bumps and wrinkles in your paper, for as it dries out it will shrink back to its original size, and because the edges are gummed to your board it will become more and more taut and, finally, extremely smooth and flat. One word of warning: when putting on the gummed strips make sure they adhere by carefully nursing the paper with your thumb in a series of gentle pressures, not by running gaily from one end to the other, for such casual treatment will probably pleat your paper at one corner and cause a most annoying wrinkle on an otherwise perfectly flat sheet. Only if the paper is very stout and heavy can it be safely used unstretched without fear of buckling. Cartridge paper is not usually made in this weight.

Now for the charcoal and wash drawing. On the newly stretched paper make your charcoal study according to the method previously explained. The only point worth remembering is that we shall endeavour to use a slightly lighter touch. The darks will still be dark but not truly the blackest of black, the reason for this being that when colour is placed over them we want it to show, and not be dulled by too much charcoal underneath. So perhaps we could say that although all parts of our charcoal drawing are in complete harmony it is 'painted' in a slightly higher key. Fix it and make sure it does not smudge. If it does, give it an extra spraying with the fixative.

Before we tint over the charcoal sketch it will be wiser if we curb our enthusiasm for the moment and indulge in a little experiment or two which will familiarise us with the contents of our new colour-box. All we need is a few odd pieces of paper, our paint-box, some water, and the large brush. Dip the brush into the water and transfer a little pool of liquid into one of the depressions in the lid of the paint-box. Then gently agitate the colour you have chosen until the brush is well loaded with paint. Mix this thoroughly into the pool of water, making quite sure the brush is free from any tiny patches of undiluted paint. We now have a supply of wet colour into which we can dip. Have your paper at a slight slant—a book under the drawing-board will do— so that you are working on a slightly inclined plane similar to an old-fashioned desk-top. Boldly, and with a fully-charged brush, put a firm horizontal stroke across the top of the paper. Try not to be timid, and endeavour to use most of the length of the hairs of the brush. The resulting brush stroke should be an even band of colour some three-eighths of an inch wide. You will notice that the colour tends to collect in a thin watery line at the base of this stroke, but this is immediately absorbed as you make the second stroke—again with a fully-charged brush. To remove this wetness at the end of the area to be painted, wipe the brush until it is almost dry, and a further gentle stroke will lift the wetness.

This is known as 'laying down a wash' and is an absolutely indispensable technique for water-colour painting. Practise it on several sheets of paper until you have the feel of it, and do use plenty of water. In *Figure* 12a and b, page 17, you will see an example of a successful wash with wet colour and in *Figure* 12c the rather scrub-like appearance when the brush is much too dry.

To Start You Painting

Back then to our charcoal sketch, over which we are going to lay these washes of colour. Our task is reasonably simple, as we only have to use a general colour—the lights and darks are already in place. There is no definite rule where to begin, but I usually start at the top and work down. This does not mean that we cannot return to a previously painted passage if we feel it needs further attention, but I must stress that it is generally better to work directly and freely and to resist strongly the temptation to 'touch up' parts that have already been painted. Various thoughts will come to you as you work; at times you will wait for an area to dry before proceeding with the one next to it; at other times you will happily let one colour flood into and blend with another. It is by these experiences that our knowledge increases, and with a charcoal and wash drawing we can take a few liberties because we know we have a good tone drawing underneath to hold the whole thing together. In my sketch of Hastings you will notice that there is a blending of wet paint on the sunny side of the old buildings, where yellow ochre and green have merged. A similar effect has been used in the ground colours where the shadows and the sunlit shingle meet. I have also made use of the blending of *damp* colours, which is very helpful, for although it retains the correct shape of things it prevents the rather stark appearance of a hard, brittle edge. It helps to keep a feeling of softness and of delicate lighting which is true to the effect of atmosphere on objects out of doors. This can be seen where the rooftops meet the hillside, and also in parts of the reflections.

What I am trying to convey is the wonderful quality of water-colour paints. They are soft and flowing; they merge and blend; they can be both firm and delicate, strong and gentle: contrasting qualities which should be made use of. I am sure you will agree that it is quite wrong to confine them into stiff, hard patches of brittle, half-dry colour. Give them scope and freedom, particularly in these charcoal-and-wash drawings, and you will create pictures of distinction and beauty.

Artists, like everyone else, speak little of their failures. If, whilst on this path towards landscape painting, you occasionally lose your way and turn out work that is dirty and muddy, do not despair, for you will be in quite good company. Failures happen to us all, but if you can come back smiling, even if a little grimly, you will find the mistakes getting less and less and your knowledge and ability growing step by step. Remember not to tackle too much too soon. Look for subjects you feel you can manage, and content yourself at this stage with 'studies' rather than 'pictures'. You will find, of course, that a really good study *is* a picture. In *Figure* 14, page 19, are two of the sort of studies which I consider would be helpful.

Finally, although I have used the charcoal-and-wash method as a stepping-stone, do not put it to one side as being merely a stunt for beginners. It just so happens that I consider its use to be progressive; but it is also a well-established method of painting, and one which can be most expressive and profound. Long after you have read this chapter I hope you will use it again and again.

At this stage you will find your critical powers developing, and you will be dissatisfied with certain passages in your work. Do not despair, as this is a very good sign of real progress. A small sketch book into which you can enter lots of reference drawings is the answer, and by continual practice you will find that you are, by your own efforts, solving the problems that these difficult passages presented.

4

Monochrome Painting

HAVING NOW HAD some experience of our paints by practice washes and by floating such washes over a charcoal drawing, the next step is to work with the pigment only. This means that the paint must be mixed and applied at varying degrees of strength to give reality to the light and dark areas of our work. Remember the terms 'weak' and 'strong', for you will often hear them. In water-colour a weak colour is one where so much water is introduced that the colour is considerably reduced. On the other hand a strong colour is one where plenty of paint is added, and although the mixture is still very fluid the colour content is considerably higher. If you think of strong and weak tea it helps to establish this in your memory. Let us suppose we are painting in one colour only—that is, in monochrome—and that we are using a very dark brown. By adding water we can weaken this colour considerably, and we might be tempted to say it was now a light colour. Actually the *colour* has not been changed, but only its *strength*. We can have light colours such as yellow and dark colours such as prussian blue, yet both light or dark colours can be painted at varying degrees of strength.

As we are now working with paint only, this is the time to find out more about paper. Previously we have used cartridge paper, but as you have seen from the illustration of charcoal rubbings there are many other kinds. The one which is probably the most well known to water-colourists is a paper known as Whatman. This is made in three surface finishes. The first is one that is left with its natural texture, which is slightly coarse and has a certain roughness. It is not pressed or rolled after it has been made and is therefore listed in the artist's catalogues as 'Whatman NOT'. This is the most popular. You will also see before it a rather mysterious number such as '90 lb', '120 lb', '140 lb', etc. This refers to its weight per ream of 480 sheets. Thus a sheet of '200 Whatman NOT' would be a fairly heavy paper with a moderately coarse surface. The other surfaces are 'H.P.', which means 'hot-pressed', and in consequence the surface is much smoother; and 'rough', which is a very coarse grain. Paper up to 120 lb weight needs stretching, but beyond this one can paint direct. Paper can be bought in blocks or pads of various sizes, or by the sheet, which usually measures 22 in. by 30 in. This is known as an Imperial Sheet.

Having obtained a few small pieces of Whatman paper (a block of 90 lb NOT, about 9 in. by 7 in., would be fine), the next step is to practise graduated washes of colour. This means starting at the top of the paper with a colour at full strength and bringing it down slowly to its palest tint. The idea is that as you proceed down the paper, remembering to have the drawing-board tilted, the brush is replenished with less and less colour but more and more water, until at the last stage the brush is being dipped only into the water.

Ultramarine is an excellent colour to begin with, for the result of a graduated wash in this colour will be a perfect example of painting a clear blue sky. There will be a strong blue at the top, representing the sky overhead, and the colour will decrease in strength just as a sky does in nature, until at the horizon there is only the slightest suggestion of colour. Thus you will have painted a truly dome-like sky. Should this surprise you, look out of the window on a good clear day and this dome-like quality will be easily observed. I can see such a sky now as I write.

After becoming proficient in laying down these graduated washes, a few experiments would be a good idea. Try, for instance, putting in a faint range of hills about halfway down the paper. Apply it first on an initial wash that is still a little damp, then on another wash that has thoroughly dried. You will have two distinct effects, which can be added to your store of experience and used later. After painting the hills, try reversing the graduated wash so that the colour gets stronger and stronger as you come down. You will now have the effect of land coming to your feet. A further experiment would be a slightly uneven stroke to suggest the broken nature of the ground. Do not attempt to scrub backwards and forwards, but float the colour across the paper in one direction, and never go up and down with the strokes—a common bad habit at this stage.

In *Figure* 15, page 20, you will see examples of these experiments, and some have been taken even further than our previous suggestion, for over them I have painted a few details to help the composition. Plenty of practice is needed, for water-colour is by no means an easy medium and it is only by learning its delightful qualities at first hand that progress will come. Experiment and make mistakes, for in the process you will have one of those breathtaking lucky accidents, and a new way of expressing something in paint will be added to your list of abilities.

The next stage is to put the knowledge gained to the test out of doors. As we are going to paint in monochrome, the first thing to bear in mind is that the colour used must be one that has a sufficient range to give us all the tones we require. Payne's Grey would be admirable. Make sure that you have an adequate supply before setting out, and check the rest of your painting and personal equipment too. Many an artist has felt very sheepish to find, when he unpacked his bag, that a most essential item had been forgotten.

Let us imagine that we are in the Lake District and that we see the scene reproduced in *Figure* 17. Our first thought, having decided on the viewpoint, would be as to how we are going to tackle the painting, and I would suggest

Figure 17. *Study in monochrome*

that we sit down quietly and think out the problems. We must decide how much of this delightful scene can be included, how much will be firmly stated and what will be hinted at in a subtle way. Can we paint every twig? What would be the best way to suggest those mountains? These and other questions must be asked and answered before the actual painting begins, because once we start we want the whole thing to proceed with a swing and a flourish, and with no timid hesitation.

First, we shall probably have to pencil in very lightly the shapes of the various masses on a quarter-Imperial sheet. Accuracy should be aimed at, but not detailed drawing, because as we paint we also draw. The brush not only puts on the paint, but is also a very sensitive drawing instrument, and can often suggest with a delicate flick what would be almost impossible with a pencil.

Now for the painting. The colour should be mixed, ready to be strengthened or weakened, and with a well-loaded brush the sky should be quickly painted in. In this picture I would recommend that the sky in the first instance be brought right down over the area occupied by the mountains, making sure that the colour is very weak behind the trees to give the effect of a haze. The mountains should be painted before this first wash is quite dry, giving them the impression of going up and over. Whilst still wet, the lighter side of the nearest

28

STAGE I

Apply the first washes, working from light to dark. Whenever possible, keep the work wet.

STAGE II

Keeping the work wet to retain a feeling of foliage, apply the darks. When the work is not quite dry, put in branches and extra darks.

THE MEASLE TOUCH

Resist the temptation to suggest separate leaves; it makes the work spotty and un-sympathetic to your material.

Figure 18—see page 36

Accent on Yellow

Accent on Blue

Accent on Brown

Colour Chart
Showing the variations
obtained by the use
of only three colours

Figure 19—see page 35

Chart showing that differing strengths of varied colours
❖ are needed to register the same value of tone ❖

Figure 20—see page 37

Figure 21. Quick sketches made with three colours—see page 37

mountain could be lifted out and the dark areas be painted into the wet paint. Already we shall have observed that it is important to assess how wet or how damp to have the painting before adding the next passage. The distant belt of trees should also be introduced whilst the painting is still wet.

Even at this early stage it will be apparent that by using our paints in this sympathetic way we are getting a better effect than if we tried to introduce any details of individual rocks or trees. We have established distance.

Next come the gentle tones of the water and at the same time the weakest passages in the rocks. These should be followed by other passages of stronger tones, which can be dropped into wet colour, taking care at this stage not to suggest the outcrop of rocks or anything that has a firmer edge. These ought to come when the work is a little drier, but the soft ripples in the water could be carefully brushed in while we are waiting.

Lastly would come the strong areas, which are carefully painted after considering how wet or dry should be the surface which receives them. Such items as the trees and the breakwater should be painted on a surface which is reasonably dry, and possibly with these it would be wise to use the smaller brush. Notice the slight weakening of tone as the trees recede.

A last look around the painting for any final touches (but take care—no fidgeting), and the work is complete—your first monochrome painting. Date it for further reference, as it will be a valuable guide to your progress. Do plenty of these sketches: they are useful practice. You will be in very good company, for most artists do the same. Not only do these monochromes help them to establish the correct tonal qualities of a scene, but they can, if done well, be truly delightful paintings.

5

The First All-Colour Painting

THE ENJOYMENT and appreciation of colour is universal, and plays a far greater role in our daily life than is often realised. Colour can excite or soothe, and even lift us to heights of real emotion. It is no accident that the strong dominance of red is used to signify danger; it is a colour which immediately catches the eye and creates an attitude of alertness. Strong and vivid colours fill us with excitement and gaiety, whilst quiet and gentle ones suggest restfulness and calm. In the hands of a competent artist colour is indeed a great vehicle for expression, and can go far beyond the mere recording of the scene before him. He can, for instance, be like the stage-designer who, without altering the scene, creates a variety of interpretations by the careful choice of coloured lighting.

There can be no doubt that in painting colour can be deeply expressive, and can be the added ingredient which gives full flavour to our work. But it can be a dangerous ingredient—one that will, if not controlled, completely spoil that flavour. Crudity can so easily appear if colour is used without a true understanding of all the other fundamentals that go into picture-making. I often tell my students not to be over-zealous in using too much brilliant and strong colouring at the expense of all else, for fear they may make their work look overdressed. That is why I ask you to enter the world of colour with caution and to remember that, although colour can give added charm to our work, unless we have an understanding of tones as outlined in the previous chapters it can easily destroy the balance and harmony in what would otherwise be a thoughtful piece of painting.

We must not forget that lighting and atmosphere will have their effect on colour and that such effects are only noticed after keen and careful observation. We have learnt from our charcoal studies the effect of the film of atmosphere between ourselves and distant objects. Try to imagine for a moment a painting in which this has been ignored. It shows a scene in which exactly the same green at the same strength of colour has been used for a tree in the foreground as for another some distance away. The far one is drawn smaller to show the distance, but its colour is such that it wants to join up with its much closer partner. This kind of conflict is very often apparent in the work of the amateur and I am constantly having to explain it.

To introduce you gently, our first colour work will be limited to a range of the three colours only. In this way it is hoped that the usual difficulties confronting the newcomer to painting will be overcome. The colours we shall use are:

> Cadmium Yellow
> Ultramarine Blue
> Burnt Umber

As Burnt Umber is a rather reddish-brown it will be seen that we are, in effect, working with a slight variation on the three primary colours—red, blue, yellow.

For a first exercise, make a graduated wash on a small piece of paper, starting with Ultramarine. Gradually weaken this and bring it down a little below halfway and then, while it is slightly damp, introduce a fairly weak yellow. Gradually increase the strength of the yellow, and merge a brown into it while it is still wet. From such a simple exercise you will create an impression of both the land and the sky receding into the picture. You will also have shown another very important feature of landscape painting, and that is that distant colours always appear a little bluer than they really are. Trial and error is the next step and I would suggest many of these little simple washes, which can have various details introduced to add interest. Only by handling and by constant use can you come to grips with the material being used. Try mixing colours and dropping them into damp colour which has already been applied, and study the effect. Make use of some of the earlier exercises and repeat them using only the three colours given.

It will soon become apparent that quite a range of colours can be obtained, and it is suggested that a simple colour chart as shown in *Figure* 19, page 30, should be made and kept for reference. This can be done by painting patches of the three colours side by side to show their appearance when pure. The second row shows yellow blended with brown, which gives a pleasant sunny mixture. Remember that this mixture can have a balance tipping towards either brown or yellow, giving quite a range, and that such colours can be considerably weakened by the addition of water. Next to this mixture carry out the same idea, but mix yellow with blue. From this you will obtain a variety of greens, from a very yellow-green to a deep blue-green. Immediately ideas of differing greens in the landscape come to mind. In the third row brown is mixed with blue, and from such mixture we can get a variety of browns, purples, greys and blues. Now we can take the experiment a little further by trying out various combinations of all three. In the first of this threesome mix-up, I have put in a little more yellow, in the second a little more blue, and in the third a little more brown. Naturally the exercise could be taken even further, and additional experiments are always profitable, but already we have a considerable selection of colours with which to venture forth.

So much for theorising. The real job now is to get down to the pleasant business of putting our knowledge to the test. Take out your equipment and let us search for a simple tree study such as the one illustrated in *Figure* 18, I and II, page 29. After a careful look at the subject we must think how to suggest it with the materials we have to hand. A quick glance at the third illustration should be enough to show that our materials are unsuited to a detailed or spotty effect. Such treatment only tends to agitate and worry the eye, and the soft dignity of the tree is lost. Obviously the sponge-like look of the foliage is better suggested by a watery application of the paint with only a few drier touches here and there.

In order to obtain such a watery look the first thing to do, after lightly pencilling in the shapes, is to prepare a good supply of two or three greens—otherwise one stage of the painting might dry before the next colour was ready. As the painting proceeds, these colours can be added to and altered. For this study a yellow-green, a brown-green and a blue-green should be mixed and ready in the wells of the paint-box. Observing that the light is from the left we will very simply suggest the background, making quite sure it is weak enough in colour not to jump forward and being careful not to let it run over any area which needs to be very light. Taking a good brushful of our yellow-green, paint the lighter areas of *one* of the clumps of foliage and while it is still wet drop in the darker side. Should it run in too much, a dry brush will lift it and tell us just what degree of dampness will give the desired effect. Branches can be suggested quite early and thus we shall work down our paper quite quickly, letting the paint run and blend as much as we can without destroying the effect we are after.

Having got the paper covered, we can now quickly view the work as a whole, and decide when and where to place any additional strokes which need to be added when the work is a little drier—such as the extra dark area on the bank, the dark patches in the water, and the mere suggestion of modelling in the tree. A few dry strokes in the branches, and you will have your sketch.

You will, I am sure, have found not only that we have been using all our previous knowledge of tone and colour mixing, but that timing is most important. The time factor in water-colour painting is both its charm and its difficulty. Not only must we know what to do and how to do it, but when. Should the paper be wet, damp or dry? This is a question that must be constantly in our mind. For your guidance may I say that the wet or damp effect usually looks best, but naturally it must be controlled. A further tip is that a gradual blending rather than a complete merging occurs on damp paper, and this dampness can be estimated by waiting for the shine of the water to disappear.

Now a word about tone and colour. Often the transfer from monochrome to colour causes some confusion, and our artistic vocabulary also becomes confused, making communication difficult. It was stated in a previous chapter that tones tend to merge as the scene recedes, and this of course is true, but because colours register different tones, it is quite possible for a distant object to be lower in tone than a near one of a different colour. For example, a yew tree in the distance could, because of its strong colour, be lower in tone than a privet hedge in the foreground. A look at the chart in *Figure* 20, page 31, will explain this. The areas marked are approximately the same tone value (that is, they would, if photographed, register the same tone of grey), but they are obviously of a different *strength* of colour. On the other hand we could easily speak of two colours being of the same strength but of a different tone value.

Lastly, *Figure* 21, page 32, shows four little quick studies which were made with the three recommended colours. I think you will agree that the results are quite pleasing and (as in most practice work) the use of this limited palette, besides being helpful as a stage in our painting progress, gives us studies which can be quite complete and satisfying.

6

The Selection and Arrangement of Subjects

I F A HOUSEWIFE brings home a bunch of flowers to decorate the home, she will be lucky indeed if she finds that, by merely unwrapping them and sticking them in a vase, an arrangement has been created which is exactly what she wants. It is much more likely that the group will require a little lift here, a twist or two there, to make it a piece of decoration which will give her satisfaction. Note that she first *selected* the variety of blooms which met with her approval and then *arranged* them into a satisfactory group.

We should do well to follow her method in preparing for our next painting: first deciding what to include in it and then seeking a pleasing arrangement. It is these two things which an artist considers when he speaks of 'composition' in painting.

Selecting a subject is by no means as simple as it may sound, and on many occasions amateur artists have told me how difficult they have found this, particularly when they are in an area where everything is paintable and the subjects are numerous.

How, then, can elimination be made and a decision arrived at when we are seeking a subject for painting? There are two things to avoid. One is the wide open landscape consisting of simply land and sky. Unless there are some definite forms, such as trees, buildings, hedges, walls, fences, etc., which will give you a sense of scale, such scenes are much too difficult for a beginner. True, they offer few problems of drawing, but the painting requires tremendous experience. The other danger is choosing a subject which is beyond your powers of draughtsmanship. Do not try to paint what you know you cannot draw, for painting is really but another form of drawing, and such an attempt will surely lead to disaster.

No one can ever say exactly what the components of a picture should be, since so much depends on personal taste and interpretation, but it is hoped the foregoing advice has narrowed the choice a little. Let me assume that you have by now seen something which appeals to you, and that you are trying to decide if it is a possible subject. Were you to ask me, I would suggest you looked at it not just as a group of things, but rather as a pattern—a pattern of light and shade and a pattern of contrasting shapes. Then we would look for something else: we would look to see if things overlapped one another without becoming

38

Figure 22

Showing how an arrangement is improved by allowing its parts to overlap

unrecognisable or uninteresting. This would lead us from one part of the group to another and give the linkage which makes for unity.

The diagrams in *Figure 22* will probably help to explain this. In 'A' we have various shapes which, although quite interesting and different, are each separate, like small islands on a sea of paper. This tends to make the whole thing a little jumpy and disconnected. In 'B' we have the same elements, but now they overlap and project, giving the whole arrangement a distinctive shape of its own. In spite of the overlapping, the various shapes are still recognisable. Thus in 'B' we have managed to say a lot more than in 'A', whilst still keeping to the same basic shapes. It is more interesting and therefore a better design. All this is quite simple, but is so often forgotten when out of doors. In 'C' and 'D' the same principles have been applied to an outdoor scene. The frontal view of 'C' keeps everything rather distinct and separate, and one's eye is inclined to sweep across the paper hoping to find greater interest somewhere else. The sketch 'D' is the same scene from a different viewpoint, and the theory of overlapping has been put to use. I am sure you will agree that the house looks very inviting as it settles itself down behind the trees. The lamp-post, too, by being in front and therefore larger, helps to give a feeling of recession.

The humble viewfinder which was described earlier comes into constant use, because it helps to divorce the subject being considered from outside influences which would otherwise intrude into the scene and distract our eyes from it. As you move around to view the subject from different angles you are really doing what our housewife did with her flowers: you are altering the arrangement. Often it is a delightful surprise to see how different the same scene can be, when seen from a changed viewpoint.

Another essential to composition is knowing where to place the main features. Nearly always it is best to avoid having our main centre of interest in the very middle of the paper. This *seems* to be the most obvious place, but to choose it will generally make all the rest of the picture look uninteresting. In *Figure 23* you will see that I have ruled up the paper as if to play noughts and crosses. You may remember that it is often a good plan to start this game off with a cross in the centre, but I hope that the cross in this case will indicate that it is wrong in the vast majority of pictures. The same is true of putting a vertical or horizontal feature halfway across or halfway up the paper. Usually it will simply cut the work in two.

Our paper ruled into thirds (both vertically and horizontally) will serve to remind us of a very important aspect of composition. If the main features fall near one of the verticals and one of the horizontals you will find the arrangement is nearly always one that gives pleasure. This point of intersection can be called the centre of interest, and it will of course come a little to one side or other of our previously noted danger spot. This is not an exact rule, because happily there are not hard and fast rules in painting and we all find that we are always learning a little more. It is rather in the nature of an aid, to help us to

The use of "Thirds"

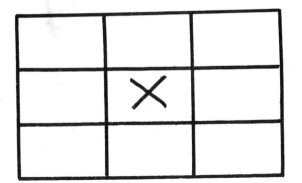

X marks the danger spot in picture composition. Dividing lines help because......

... one of the verticals and one of the horizontals usually cuts through the main features

Figure 23

arrange a picture that will satisfy. You may be interested to know that it is an approximation to the 'Golden Rule' or 'Golden Mean', a mathematical formula similar to our 'thirds' which has been applied by mathematicians to many of the paintings of the old masters, and has proved to be surprisingly accurate. However, I am quite sure these artists never worked out their masterpieces with a slide rule : their successes were created merely by a feeling that what they had done looked 'right'.

With the knowledge of these aids to composition we should now be well-armed to find countless subjects. In fact subjects can be found everywhere, and you will join company with Constable, that wonderful landscape painter, who, when asked by a lady if he did not consider the subject he was painting to be rather ugly, replied, 'Madam, nothing is ever ugly.'

It has already been stated how extremely useful is our viewfinder, but equally important is the small sketch which enables us to see how our chosen scene looks on paper. Always make plenty of sketches, and by this I mean serious little notes of shape, form and colour. Only when experience enables you to see the picture in your mind's eye, will it be safe to dispense with a preliminary sketch.

Another problem which often puzzles the newcomer to painting is the difficulty of transferring the approved small sketch onto a bigger piece of paper.

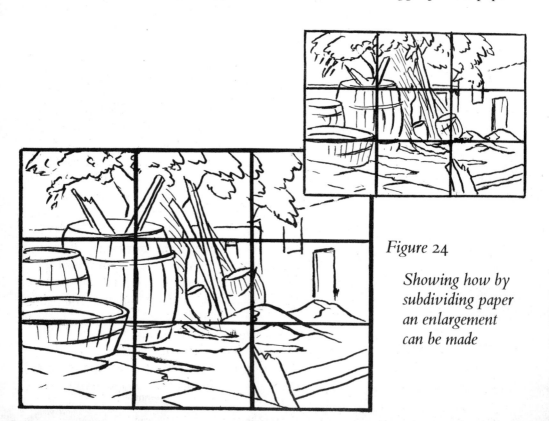

Figure 24

Showing how by subdividing paper an enlargement can be made

The Selection and Arrangement of Subjects

The sheet suddenly seems frighteningly large and empty, and we are filled with all kinds of doubts. If the enlargement is done hurriedly we often get our proportions wrong, and find that all sorts of extra details have crept in around the subject—details which were not in our original sketch. *Figure* 24 explains a very simple method of enlarging, by once more dividing both our small sketch and the larger sheet of paper into thirds. By observing where the lines of the small sketch cross, follow, and wander away from the lines of the 'thirds', it is possible to make the same strokes in corresponding places on the bigger paper. The two sketches will thus be in proportion to each other. The only point to watch is that both sheets must be similar in shape: obviously one cannot change a square into an oblong and still have an accurate enlargement.

Perspective! The very word seems to frighten the would-be artist. This is a great pity, for it is a fascinating subject and one which should not be shirked, for in one form or another it comes into every painting. In this book my aim is to give a few hints which have proved helpful in the past and which will, I hope, remove some fears and lead you on in search of further knowledge.

To encourage you, perhaps I can be forgiven for including a little personal story. My wife was also, at one time, a little scared of any subject which contained a fair amount of perspective drawing. She accepted only minor challenges in this direction, until one holiday when we were painting in Oxford. Suddenly all the preparation in previous work bore fruit, and she found great satisfaction in painting scenes which took in parts of the architectural splendour of this delightful city. Now she loves the subject which once scared her.

The basic fact of perspective is that what we know are parallel lines on, let us say, a building, appear to be at an angle or a slope when viewed from any position other than one directly facing it. This can be seen by looking again at the building in *Figure* 22. In 'C' all the lines across the house are horizontal, whereas in 'D' they appear to converge as the further parts of the building recede. It is essential, when making a drawing of this sort, to get at least two of these angles down accurately. The rest will follow. I usually endeavour to establish one line at the base and one near the top, as these show the greatest difference in direction. Although it sounds foolish, many of us find difficulty in deciding exactly which way a certain feature tips, and we find ourselves wondering which end of it goes up and which goes down. A simple method of finding out is to hold a fairly long pencil between the finger-tips of each hand. If it is kept at arm's length, and perfectly level, it can be brought up slowly until it appears to touch some important corner—say the end of the eaves in *Figure* 25A. It then becomes immediately apparent which way the roof seems to tip.

An extension of such a seeing-aid is a gadget which can be made quite simply with two strips of fairly stiff card joined by a paper-fastener. You then have two long arms which swivel open like the blades of scissors, with the joint stiff enough for the arms to stay fixed in any position. *Figure* 25B shows

Figure 25

Angles can be observed by holding a pencil horizontally between the finger-tips

HORIZONTAL

HORIZONTAL

Two pieces of card with a firm but movable joint, help to transfer difficult angles from scene to paper

it in use. One arm is marked 'horizontal' and must always be in that position. The other is moved until it appears to run along the feature to be drawn. Make quite sure the device is held 'square' to the body, and you will then have the correct angle, which can be very easily compared with your drawing.

In an earlier chapter it was established that similar objects appear to decrease in size as they recede into the distance. To help to compare the different sizes of various objects, a very simple sliding scale can be improvised by moving the thumb-tip along a pencil. This can be held at any angle and the comparative sizes can be studied by noting the distance between the thumb-tip and the end of the pencil, as shown in *Figure* 26. Be absolutely certain when using it to keep the arm fully outstretched, as otherwise the comparison is untrue and the idea is useless. Keep a good straight arm and the scale of things will be recorded with ease and accuracy.

With these few hints your painting should progress quite satisfactorily, but such aids are only a small part of a most interesting study. As you improve you will want to know more, and then it will be time to delve a little more deeply.

Figure 26. *A sliding gauge made with thumb and pencil is a simple method of deducing relative sizes*

7

Colours at our Command

TONE IS MORE IMPORTANT than colour! This well-known statement often causes confusion, but as I consider it to be utterly true and most important to the understanding of this difficult business of painting, I feel it must be fully appreciated. When dealing with our simple three-colour palette of yellow, blue and brown, it was found that these colours each had a different tone value when painted at full strength, and that such values could be altered by the inclusion of more water. We found, too, that perfectly adequate interpretations of a subject could be made with only one colour, as in the monochrome sketches, and that even with only three colours, quite profound and expressive work could be done, which lost little of its appeal through the limitation of colour. Any success that was gained was achieved not by the use of bright and varied colour, but by the understanding of tone. Franz Hals, whose work is so sparkling and alive, painted many of his most famous portraits with the use of only four colours!

Colour, therefore, is the *extra* jewel which can give an added sparkle and quality to our work, but like all forms of decoration it must be respected and understood and never overdone. In painting it must be used in conjunction with and after consideration of things like shape, form, tone and composition. Imagine a beautiful woman in a well-cut gown who is so bedecked with buttons, bows, posies, clips, clasps, jabots, brooches, bangles and beads, that the beauty of the gown is obscured. All those extra decorations not only hide the thing of real beauty, but are so confusing that whatever attraction each piece may have is lost in the conflict for our attention. The lady is overdressed. So it is with colour. It can be a great aid to our paintings, by giving them extra richness and quality, but it must be used with discretion and as a part of a whole.

Having, I hope, made my point, let us see what subtle delights the use of extra colours can offer. You will remember that in Chapter 3 I gave a list of colours which were recommended as being adequate for most purposes. For easy reference, this list is repeated here:

> Two yellows—Cadmium Yellow, Yellow Ochre
> Two reds   —Vermilion, Alizarin Crimson
> One brown —Burnt Umber
> One blue   —Ultramarine
> One green   —Viridian
> One grey   —Payne's Grey

Newcomers to painting often express surprise at the small number of colours recommended. If you also are surprised, and perhaps a little doubtful, let me reassure you that for the vast majority of our paintings these colours will, with a little mixing, give us everything we need. May I beg you not to succumb to the persuasion of some keen salesman and arrive home with one of those enormous boxes filled with dozens of colours. The largest box ever made would never be adequate, as it stood, for every occasion. What is more, it would spoil your enjoyment by taking from you the fun and excitement of discovering new and unusual mixtures. Worse still, it would rob your work of its individuality by always trying to force you to accept the 'ready-made' answer to any colour problem, and this in turn would discourage the absorbing and instructive habit of truly searching for colour. These huge boxes are also too cumbersome to carry and too heavy to hold.

The chart (*Figure* 28, pp. 50 and 51) shows an experiment in the mixing and blending of colours. From it can be found what happens when any two colours are mixed together. By painting each part in a very moist and fluid way a variety of effects can be observed, many of them creating exciting and subtle colours. Only seven of the eight colours have been used: Payne's Grey was excluded, as we are going to deal with that separately. It is seriously recommended that you make a chart like this and carry it in your sketch-bag, where it will be at hand to give help and reference when working out of doors. All you need is a sheet of quarter-Imperial paper (15 in. by 11 in.), ruled out to give seven divisions descending in seven steps. In the first row place little dabs of colour, a different one for each of the divisions, starting with Cadmium Yellow. In the second row, Cadmium Yellow is mixed with the remaining colours in the top row, treating each division in turn. The third row is the turn of Yellow Ochre, and so on in decreasing steps.

When painting a picture, the colours are usually mixed in the depressions of the palette attached to the paint-box, but in this case, as I wanted to observe the mixture made by varying proportions of two colours, I allowed the paints to run freely together whilst on the paper, and whilst both were quite wet. No attempt was made to tidy up the shape, as it was the freely mixing quality I wished to observe. Thus the two colours merge and blend where the two arms of the 'V' meet. Then, to see the effect of a weaker mixture, water was added and the V was 'washed' down to make a Y. Complete the chart as I have done and, in addition to improving your facility for handling the materials, you are due for some pleasant surprises. The delightful variation of colours of great subtlety that comes from the mixing of Crimson with Viridian is a fine example—and just look at the variety of greens that can be made.

Examine carefully the areas where two colours meet, for if you have kept the work clean and rather wet, it is here that small blurred patches of about four differing mixtures will be seen. Thus in each of the twenty-one mixtures there will be at least four variations, which gives us a selection of more than eighty-four colours, plus our original seven. This is a considerable range, but the story is by no means concluded, as we have made no attempt to mix more than two colours at any one time. Try making a chart with mixtures of three colours, and the beginnings of a palette of infinite scope are within your grasp.

Experiment like mad. You will find all sorts of surprises, delights—and sometimes disappointments. As you progress, try mixing colours in the orthodox way in the palette, adding a little colour at a time. Some mixtures will be wonderful and then, with the merest touch of something already used, the mixture becomes a hippopotamus special—mud! Try it again, altering the proportions of the mixture. You may still have a greyish hue, but this time it is one with a gentle hint of colour, and you have found something that had previously been elusive.

Until you are fairly experienced I would not advise mixing more than three colours. The important thing is to experiment by trial and error, remembering that the man who never made a mistake never made anything. By experience you will remember the mixtures more easily, and (what is equally important) you will get a sureness and speed which is a great asset. It is most disappointing to find that, having taken so long to get the desired mixture, the part of your painting which you hoped to catch while still damp, has dried, and what was to have been a pleasant feathery edge has become a hard and brittle line.

In the first of the three sketches in *Figure* 27, opposite, I have painted a scene in fairly true colours, making use of some of the mixtures made in the chart. You will notice how the colours become warmer (there is a little red in them) as the scene advances, and cooler (there is blue in them) as it recedes. Use has been made of the blending effect of placing two wet colours together which was also observed when making the chart. This little sketch also shows that not only is there a drawing lightly done in pencil to serve as a reminder of the various shapes, but there is quite a lot of brush drawing too.

The second sketch makes further use of the knowledge that colours are cooler in the background. The trees and all beyond them are very blue in colour, whilst all in front of them is very much a story of reds and yellows. I think you will agree it is quite a pleasant interpretation and such a method, with many variations, can be used to great advantage if, in your opinion, the actual colours of the scene are unpleasant or do not have harmony. In such a case use the composition, but not the colour. Never be scared of experimenting with colour. By all means work hard to develop the ability to match any colour you see. This does not mean, however, that you have to accept exactly what is before you just because it is there.

The third sketch makes use of the 'colour wheel' shown on page 51. If the three basic or primary colours are set down as equal segments of a circle it will be found that where they merge an extra colour is created. This is called a secondary colour. Thus from yellow, red and blue can be made orange, green and violet. By using this circular arrangement it can be seen that opposite each

SKETCH A

This sketch uses the mixtures that can be obtained from the Colour Chart in Figure 28

SKETCH B

By using mainly reds and blues, this interpretation shows that blue recedes and red advances

SKETCH C

By using complementary or opposite colours, a harmonious interpretation can be made. The colours used here were yellow and violet; red and green

Figure 27

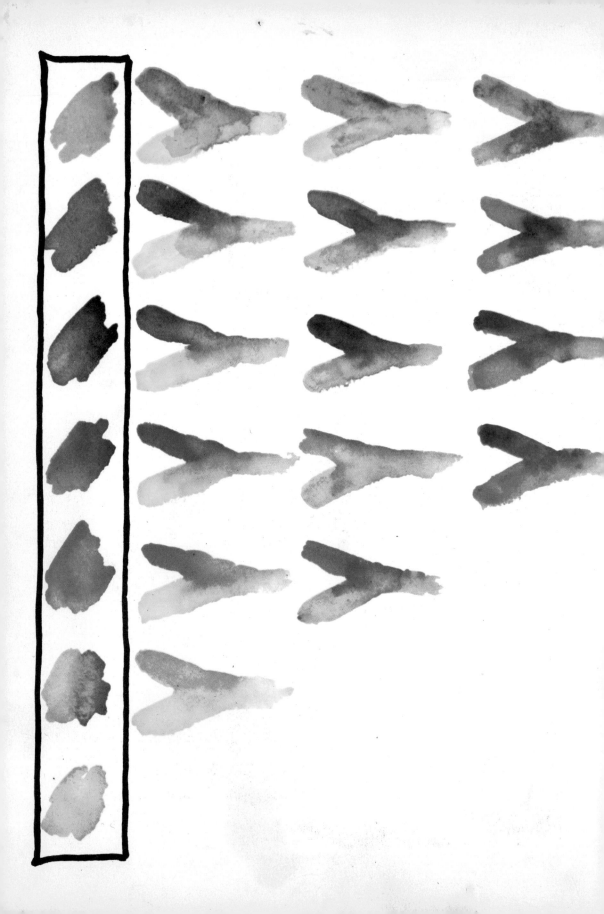

primary colour appears a secondary colour. Each pair of opposites so represented contains colours which are complementary to each other; therefore yellow and violet are complementary colours. This elementary piece of theory is very useful, for such pairs of colours will always make the basis of a harmonious combination. The third sketch has the violet and yellow combination as its main theme, and combined with it is the red and green harmony, making a colourful picture which is indicative of the atmosphere of the scene. The changes made are not too revolutionary, but they are sufficient to prove helpful when you wish to make changes of colour and yet feel uncertain. In such circumstances, remember the colour wheel.

In the last two sketches some liberties were taken. They are merely examples to show what can be done when a change is considered necessary because of some local colour problem or because a certain interpretation is desired. Fortunately such problems are rather rare because nature is very kind, and time, wind, rain and sunshine have a delightful way of blending and unifying. Nevertheless a personal approach is of supreme importance and I hope my examples have set you thinking about colour and made you keen to learn more about it for yourself.

8

Trees, Foliage and Grass

TREES ARE AMONG the most beautiful of all living things and it is not surprising that they have for so long been the source of inspiration to writers, poets, musicians—and artists—offering, as they do, enormous scope and a great challenge to all who desire to express their many beauties. Their importance in the landscape cannot be over-emphasised, for they are probably the loveliest feature in any composition. Imagine a London square without its plane trees, Cambridge without its drooping, shady willows, or a Cotswold farm with no sheltering and protecting elms, and the importance of trees is strikingly emphasised. Gentle, soft and feathery shapes provide delicate and decorative silhouettes; trunks and branches provide a crisp contrast to the rhythmic curves of the masses of foliage, presenting us with a scene so gracious that it pleads to be painted.

Observed with the fresh eye of the explorer, trees can offer a great deal. They present pattern and ever-changing colour, texture, strength, nobility, delicacy —and even grotesqueness. From the heaven-searching poplars, the feathery willows and the almost oriental Scots pine, to the massive protective dignity of the oak or the chestnut, we discover an enormous wealth of information and variety which is hard to find in any other subject.

Believing sincerely that we are directing our energies to something eminently worth-while, we must now consider how to record these beautiful objects in some tangible way. Like all things that are really worth doing, tree painting bristles with difficulties; but that should provoke no despondency, for therein lies the pleasure and the fun. Nobody derives real or lasting satisfaction from doing what anybody else can do with ease. The problems create the pleasure. Obviously, then, the problems must be tackled carefully, and my task is to direct you to an intelligent and sympathetic approach to the drawing and painting of trees.

The best policy is a step-by-step advance, for it would be foolish if we rushed for our colour box without first having some understanding of how to proceed and what to look for. The actual business of putting paint to paper is not very difficult; it is the problem of what to include and what to discard that causes the artist to ponder. Too often the beginner who rushes at the subject in a burst of enthusiasm finds that the painting gets out of control, and the result is bitterly disappointing. So beware of over-enthusiasm and make haste slowly.

Trees, Foliage and Grass

Were I your artist-tutor on a painting holiday, I would at this stage take you and the rest of the party for a ramble. No equipment would be carried, as our intention would be merely to 'read' the landscape story. In other words, we would set out to translate subjects into simple terms, so that our mind was clear before the actual painting was begun. This is our thinking time, during which we are making observations and deciding how the various problems which confront us can be simplified and unified in order to translate the subject into the terms of water-colour painting. This is very important. A famous artist was once asked, in my hearing, how long it took him to complete a particular painting. His reply was: 'About three hours' work and twenty-five years' thought.' He was, apart from being a little facetious, trying to force home the necessity of adequate preparation and observation.

On our walk the first thing to observe would be the silhouette of a tree (or trees) as a mass. Always try to see things not as an outline but as a mass of fairly solid tone. This has been done in the sketch in *Figure* 30a. Having such an image in mind will immediately create an impression of solidity and will tend to bring the tree away from its background. Shape alone, however helpful it may be, will not give sufficient information for us to begin painting. The great temptation now is to look for all kinds of unnecessary detail. It is a temptation which must be sternly resisted, as what we need is essentials. There would be little point in counting all the leaves and painting them, if we found that we still had not managed to capture the protective and embracing rotundity of the tree. Rather than search for insignificant tiny items, let us now look within the solid masses for the large clusters of foliage which go to make up the whole area. Think of these clusters as green sponges on stalks, like those effective little trees that can be seen in an architect's model, for that is exactly how they are made. Each cluster will have its own ration of light and shade, and each has the ability to cast a shadow which may affect adjacent foliage. This image is illustrated in *Figure* 30b.

From these two images the tree can now be visualised as if painted—*Figure* 30c. Notice how the edges have been blended to have a softening effect, and that the various tones range from white to a very low tone indeed. The outside edge of the main shape has also been 'chattered' to suggest leafiness. This is very important, for no tree has a silhouette so smooth that it appears to be a cut-out shape. Such an appearance is exactly what we wish to avoid, as most trees blend into their setting and seldom appear stark and brittle.

All that has been written so far about trees is equally true in relation to other types of foliage and grass. When dealing with grass, first establish the main area and then break that area down into the shapes made by the most important clumps. Each of these will have its own light and shade, and the result will prove far more satisfactory than trying to make hundreds of strokes to represent the countless blades. If the latter method is used, even the most painstaking work merely looks like a flat wall decorated with lots of little strokes.

Figure 30

a. *When observing trees, look for the general silhouette rather than for a lot of detail*

b. *Within the silhouette look for the main shapes of the largest masses of foliage*

c. *Keen observation of shape and general masses will translate the scene into terms such as this*

d. *Before painting, keep the drawing to a minimum, as further drawing is done with a brush*

By now we probably have a fair idea of what to put into our tree study. I would suggest making a few monochrome studies, as I have done in *Figure* 30d. First comes the pencil sketch, which serves to indicate the position of our tree and also reminds us of the placing of the smaller areas and the various accents which we have decided are important. At this stage there is always a temptation to over-draw, but hold on to the visualised interpretation as illustrated and only draw what is essential to your desired result. Do not misunderstand me: preliminary drawing is absolutely essential and some mere nebulous scribble simply will not do; on the other hand, resist the temptation to put in a lot of niggling detail which, at best, will only confuse. Having made your pencil 'indication', now paint it in, trying to work with a fully-loaded brush of the right tone. Endeavour to estimate when to put one tone onto another. If the work is too wet it will 'run', but with a little practice you will soon get the feel of things and know when to work with the paper wet and when to wait until it is merely damp. Occasionally a few crisp touches can be made when the work is dry, but have care: this is the point when so often we get carried away, and freshness is lost at the expense of over-decoration of detail.

Assuming that this preparatory work has been done diligently—and, I trust, with great enjoyment and satisfaction—now is the time to enter the luscious land of colour. At first glance all the trees, grass and foliage seem overpoweringly green, but here again our little ramble of observation has helped. If we were truly looking we would have noticed a tremendous variety of greens. Some were warm greens, some cold; some were purple greens, some grey. An oak tree in summer is a grand example, for its greens range from almost yellow ochre to a rich deep purple-green. A further example is the rose bush with leaves which sometimes make one wonder whether they should be described as red or green. With beginners, a very common fault in tree painting is the use of only a light and a dark green. The introduction of grey-greens and purple-greens is imperative if the tree is to display depth and substance.

To help you, I have prepared in *Figure* 29, page 52, a chart for the making of greens which still uses our basic palette of seven colours. What I have done is to mix some viridian with each of the other colours and to add a little of each mixture to each of the colours at the top of the chart. In this way a series of greens has been made (each containing three colours), all of which can be varied by slight alterations in the proportions of the included colours. I strongly advise you to make such a chart and to study the results at first hand. To read and understand the theory is not enough; practice and experience are also needed. When the chart is complete, use the surplus colour around the paint-box for a little 'quickie', similar to the one illustrated; you will notice once again that the cold colours 'go back' and the warm colours 'come forward'. If you put down something quite casually, keeping this in mind, you will be surprised how such a quick impression will 'hold together', and it is very good practice.

To Start You Painting

In the tree study in *Figure* 31, page 61, I have made use of many of these greens, and three stages have been shown in an attempt to simplify the procedure. In Stage I the sky was painted first. I started with a thin wash of yellow ochre, and before it was quite dry a mixture of ultramarine and a little vermilion was added, dragging the brush to give a broken texture. This was changed for a very weak vermilion as it descended to the horizon. Before the background was absolutely dry the tree shape was washed in with a mixture of yellow ochre, viridian and the merest touch of vermilion. The trunk is weak vermilion and the background trees are ultramarine with a tiny spot of umber.

Stage II, which was commenced before the previous work was quite dry, shows the definition of some of the main masses by the use of viridian-ochre-crimson, taking care with the proportions to ensure the correct colour and tone. A little of the same mixture was used for the foreground and the cast shadows.

Stage III shows the inclusion of the deepest tones, which were made with viridian-ochre-umber and viridian-umber-blue. The path and the trunk were a blend of umber-vermilion, and the final accents were extra darks made with ultramarine-umber. Occasionally a little ochre, umber or purple was dropped in whilst other colours were still wet. Throughout, the brush was held very lightly so that it dragged and danced across the paper to give the work a lively and atmospheric texture.

This is the method I normally adopt, but it is by no means the only one. There are dozens of ways of scoring a goal other than the delicate fleet-footed cross-shot; there are many ways in painting. This method which I offer is one which will assist the progressing painter to attain a reasonable measure of success. With practice comes confidence and a certainty of touch which allows for countless personal interpretations.

9

The Value of Greys

WHEN AN ARTIST thinks of grey, his mind projects a much happier image than the rather drab and doleful colour that is associated with such things as prison uniforms or the mere mixing of black and white. To him, greys are subtle for they have all been influenced, however slightly, by the inclusion of colour. If this is puzzling, perhaps I can explain it in a way that often presents itself when working with students out of doors. If one of them states that a certain area, let us say a stone wall, is grey, I usually accept the remark but immediately follow it with a question something like this: 'Yes, I know it is grey; but supposing in some magical way I could remove all the black-and-white greyness. What colour would it be then?' This immediately makes him or her search for the colour content, no matter how elusive or fleeting it may be, and leads to the more neutral passages of the work remaining subdued but having much greater interest. Moreover, the colour within these areas is almost invariably of the same family as the main parts of the picture, and by absorbing some of this over-all colouring the completed work has a much greater feeling of cohesion and unity.

We have already used greys with a hint of colour, for it was found that a tinted grey could be made from such mixtures as blue-brown or green-crimson and one or two others. In the work on trees we discovered that grey-greens were essential to give a feeling of volume and rotundity. There are, however, many objects which have a natural greyness before the atmosphere and light begin their delightful tricks. Such things as various kinds of stone-work and some varieties of bricks, old and weather-beaten timber, concrete, and galvanised iron are just a few examples. In coping with such things it might cause almost insurmountable problems if we had continually to keep mixing a basic grey to which colour had to be added. Because of this, Payne's Grey has been recommended as a useful colour to include in your paint-box. Now at last it will be put to use. We shall not use it 'neat' for it is so strong that this can only be done, with great restraint, for a few incidentals. We shall, however, use it as a basis for making these subtle and delightful slightly-coloured greys which are so typical of our very lovely British landscape and which will grace our work with a dignity and restraint that cannot be obtained by using only bright and vibrant colours.

The chart in *Figure* 32, page 62, explains how to obtain some of these very pleasing colours. The first column shows the colours used and the next two columns show these colours mixed firstly with Payne's Grey and secondly with a grey made from blue-brown. The columns of greys, although very similar, are not quite the same. This gives even greater variety, but the advantage of using Payne's Grey is, of course, the saving of time. It is most frustrating to find that the mixing of three colours has taken so long that the passage waiting to be painted has dried, although we particularly wished to get to it whilst it was still damp. It is far better, if time presses, to use only two colours to get your mixture.

In the two sketches next to the chart I have made use of greys, and these serve to accentuate the bright sunlit areas. In both sketches the board was kept tilted (about 15 degrees), allowing the colours to run down one into another with no further handling. When the whole area was dry a very pale colour was dragged across the walls to create an impression of stonework.

Concentrate on greys. Whether light or dark, their quiet neutrality makes a pleasing contrast with the more colourful passages in your work, and this often allows you to paint with a refreshing simplicity.

Figure 33. Laying in the washes—see page 67

Figure 34. A later stage, when the tone values have been established

Figure 35. A group of Derbyshire cottages

Look over My Shoulder

I N THIS CHAPTER you are invited to do what the heading suggests, and look on whilst I am painting. In this way I hope to anticipate your questions and many of the problems concerning the handling of water-colour will be solved. Furthermore, such a demonstration will serve to show how the many skills and techniques can be kept together as a team working on the various parts of the picture, without losing the essential feeling for unity and harmony. Not only must each part be well done, but all parts must live happily together.

The chosen scene is shown as a finished painting in *Figure* 35, opposite, the original work measuring 14 in. by 10 in. It shows a typical piece of Derbyshire in one of the many delightful villages that can be found a few miles from Buxton. This is a rewarding area in which to work. Mountain and hill arise to cast their shadow over rich and fertile valleys, punctuated with charming little groups such as this, which are far removed from the bleakness and industrialisation which are so often associated with the Midlands. Bleakness and industrialisation can be found here too, but these also can produce the most interesting subjects.

However, we must return to our village. It is in a limestone area, and this material is widely used in rural architecture. After years of absorbing and repelling the elements it takes on a great richness which naturally blends well with the surrounding countryside. Occasionally other materials are used, but again time and weather have their softening effect, and eventually the artist is presented with an almost 'ready-made' picture.

Like all good things, the group illustrated was not easily found and was eventually discovered whilst looking around the local churchyard. A peep over the low wall, and there was this obscure back lane—almost as I have shown it. As far as I can remember, the only alteration made was to move the big tree a little to the right, as in its original position it almost appeared to grow out of the chimney. Also, by being so far to the left, it left rather an unpleasant gap between itself and the large building.

Having made myself comfortable, which is extremely important, I settled down with all my materials to hand and carefully considered the scene. The day was a little gusty, with broken cloud, so I waited until a shaft of sunlight heightened the scene, making everything much more interesting. I quickly made a mental note of the nicely-shaped shadows and proceeded with my

Figure 36

preliminary pencil sketch, which is shown in *Figure* 36. This was made after first getting the whole group to sit comfortably in the picture area as seen through my viewfinder. An ordinary HB pencil was used with quite a light touch so that the lines could, if necessary, be erased when the painting was completed. As you can see, sufficient drawing was included to help in establishing the important shapes, and such detail as needed careful painting was also put in. On the other hand the pencil work is not so detailed that it would not allow scope for additional and expressive drawing to be completed later with the brush.

Then I began to paint, starting with the sky. This is my usual approach, for if the sky can be correctly established there is immediately a point of comparison for every other part of the picture. Great care is essential here, for since you are working on a surface of glaring untouched white there is a tendency to under-estimate the amount of colour needed. It is most disappointing to paint a good sky and to find later that, in comparison with the rest of the work, it appears weak and insipid.

In this picture I noticed an ochre glow over quite a lot of the scene, and so a little ochre, very weak, was dragged into the lighter areas of the sky and washed off at the edges, and the same colour was put into other parts of the painting where it could await further attention. Before this ochre wash had dried, the sky was worked on with a mixture of ultramarine-viridian, drawing in the cloud formation with a sideways dragging stroke which left tiny areas of the paper untouched. This mixture was weakened as it got to the horizon

66

to keep the dome-like quality. Again before the area was dry, a little vermilion was added to the mixture and this was touched into the central area.

A little clean water was the next thing, as I wanted to include the fresh and very light passages that occurred. The roofs were painted in very light tones of blue, red and purple, as a foundation for extra applications of colour. The grassy banks were blocked in with a mixture of ochre plus a very little viridian, and this also served as an underpaint. Thus the work, although still very damp, was gradually taking shape and the glare of the white paper was being overcome. As previously stated, this dampness, although difficult to control, is essential, as it keeps edges soft and prevents a hard and brittle look from creeping into the scene. An example of such a soft edge is where the hills meet the sky, giving the impression that the range of hills has solidity, and not only goes up but also goes over and down. The completion of this stage is shown in *Figure* 33, page 63.

Progress was, of course, continuous, but for the convenience of demonstrating I have shown a further stage in *Figure* 34. My next step was to paint in the background of trees in the manner explained in Chapter 9, that is, by working from a general colour and gradually dropping in darker colours. These trees were painted *into* a sky which was barely dry, using mainly an ochre-viridian and umber-viridian mixture with either a little blue or a little red added to give greyness or warmth. Notice how the trees tend to darken as they go down behind the buildings. Whilst the greens were in use, the small tree was added and some of the darker parts of the grass banks were dropped in.

By now, the light colours previously painted on the buildings were practically dry. This was the time to paint the darker walls with a mixture of umber-ultramarine. As soon as it was applied a little was lifted with an almost dry brush, thus giving the effect of one colour glowing through another. The same technique was used, with subtle variations of colour, on the other buildings with a little extra colour occasionally dropped in. Thus it can be seen that in this second stage the plan was gradually to establish some of the darker areas. Extra colour was applied to the roof to suggest tiling; a shadow with a water-softened edge was placed under the eaves; the dark general tone of the garden was inserted, and the chimneys painted. All this enhanced the form of the various items and increased the effect of the lighting.

Lastly came the extra touches which gave the work its finished appearance. These can be seen by again referring to *Figure* 35, page 64. This is always the dangerous stage, for it is now that we are tempted to include lots of detail. To put in too much would destroy the beautiful broad simplicity that is the charm of a good water-colour, and would make the eye flicker and fidget instead of encouraging it to rest calmly within the picture. Therefore, with care and restraint, the windows were suggested with various blue-greys and purple-greys. An extra tile-edge or two was painted, a branch was hinted at here and there, in went the little gate and, lastly, the lovely rich foreground shadows.

To Start You Painting

To ensure a soft edge to the latter, the area of the path was treated with clean water, and the dark colours were applied before it was quite dry. The colours used for this shadow were mixtures of Payne's Grey/crimson with additions of blue or brown. Then, with great deliberation, the painting was carefully put aside to dry. Any more work, and it would have been spoiled.

★   ★   ★

Apart from the few random thoughts which follow, this is the end of my attempt to start you painting. I hope it has whetted your appetite and made you keen to continue with the delightful but difficult business of water-colour painting. At whatever stage we may be as artists, the sincere help and advice of friends and fellow-artists is of inestimable value. If this book has helped you, it will, in an indirect way, be a repayment to many people who have been generous to me with their help and encouragement. What we have achieved together in this book is only a beginning, but if you have decided to make painting your hobby you are, automatically, a member of a powerful guild of friendship whose unwritten law is that each gives freely of his talents to those interested. Thus, as you paint so do you learn, and the world is rich with ever-increasing pleasure.

Random Thoughts

N
O BOOK on water-colour painting, however comprehensive, could ever cover every aspect, and this one is no exception. Its purpose has been to help you make a start by suggesting a general direction, and thereby to enable you to steer a course clear of the many hazards which confront the beginner. There were occasions when I was tempted to include all kinds of extra information and detail, but such a plan was rejected for fear we should lose this essential direction. In this last chapter I have written down some of the many things that have been in my mind whilst writing this book. I offer them now, rather in the nature of a postscript.

First, keep the work *clean*. In a pure water-colour painting no white paint is used, and lightness and brilliance are obtained by the application of semi-transparent 'washes', or films of colour, which allow the whiteness of the paper to show through the paint. Even in very dark passages this idea of transparency must be kept in mind. The painting should never look opaque or inky and should always give the feeling that the paper beneath is doing a lot of the work by trying to peep through. Such purity can never be obtained if brushes, palette or water are dirty. Use plenty of water and change if often. Remember the old saying: 'One cannot mix with mud and come up clean.' This was obviously intended as a piece of social training, but it might equally well have been written for the water-colourist. If your mixture is muddy and colourless, and if your palette is messy, it is time to clean up all round and make a fresh start.

When out of doors make a habit of continually giving a backward glance, for the best subjects are often behind you. The habit of turning around will often reward us with the presentation of an entirely new viewpoint and may save a lot of fruitless searching.

A good general plan for the water-colourist is to work from light to dark. By keeping the water clean for the delicate areas and by restraining your enthusiasm, this method will help to retain the essential freshness of the work. Only change this plan if, by so doing, you will capture some particular effect that you wish to register as an essential yardstick of comparison for the rest of the painting.

Endeavour to paint the right tone and colour at the first attempt, and resist the temptation to keep putting one colour over another which has already dried. Superimposed paint can soon give the work a dirty appearance, and such a technique is advisable only when the desired effect can be captured in no other way. I always endeavour to get what I want with a maximum of two applications, but one is preferable. There is a method known as 'pale wash over pale wash', but it is really for the experts, and even then it is often done at the expense of freshness. The direct method is more atmospheric and less likely to go muddy.

Cheap materials cannot produce good work. It is always a source of surprise to me when I hear of someone who, on taking up a hobby such as photography, will set off cheerfully and spend a considerable amount on quite expensive materials, but when taking up painting will often use very poor quality stuff. A good artist is a craftsman too, and cannot work well with poor tools. For this reason he buys the best he can afford—and looks after them. Do as he does and keep your materials in good order. Wash and re-shape brushes after use and keep them attached to a strip of stout card with an elastic band to prevent the points from becoming bruised.

Beware of too many gadgets, particularly those which are complicated and have all manner of bits and pieces that are detachable and liable to get lost. Organise your kit as the professional does, so that there is a smooth rhythm in all you do, with the minimum of paraphernalia that can go wrong and cause frustration. For painting, our outlook must be relaxed and untroubled: the screw that will not turn, or the device that will not unfold, can play havoc with our inspiration.

Use good quality water-colour papers and experiment with the various surfaces. Heavyweight papers (above 120 lb) will not require stretching, but below this weight they will wrinkle if unstretched. A good all-purpose paper is a 90 lb Whatman NOT.

Extra colours should only be purchased after careful consideration. It may be that you have difficulty in mixing certain colours and wish to try a different approach—monastral blue and raw sienna give a beautifully rich green, for example—but never rush off and get lots of additional colours just because a certain person always uses them. Make changes gradually and, after experimenting, either accept them as a replacement or, most important, reject them if they do not suit you. Never over-load the paint-box with too many colours, but gradually sort out what is suitable for your particular temperament.

Carry a small sketch-book with you and sketch like mad at every opportunity. Do not try and make finished pictures, but use it as a personal record of things seen and observed. This will not only be extremely good practice but will serve you well as both a physical and mental record, and will slowly build itself into a vast library of information from which you can draw facts and impressions at will.

If you see something which impresses you, but are without materials, quietly absorb it and ask yourself how you would set about painting it. I call this 'painting with your eyes'. It is truly surprising how these scenes and the problems they present can be remembered, and the knowledge used when you are painting something similar.

Never purchase a stool that has little projections on the corners of the seat. The full significance of such a warning can only fully be appreciated by those who have sat on one—and then tried to stand.

Whenever possible go to the best exhibitions and study the works of those artists whose style impresses you. Look for the painting which has successfully mastered problems which you yourself found difficult, and try to understand how such difficulties were overcome. Keep your sights high, but not too high, remembering that the artist whose work you so admire also began at the beginning.

Do not seek cheap praise. It may make you feel good for a time, but ultimately it does nothing to make you stretch your talents and improve your style. On the other hand, do not allow ill-informed criticism to disturb you or cause needless uncertainty. If possible, join an Art Society, where there will be serious talks and criticisms by visiting experts, and where advice will be offered with friendship and sincerity.

When painting out of doors try to find a spot which offers a good view but does not allow the onlooker to come breathing down the back of your neck. With onlookers my advice is: never get into conversation unless you are a very steadfast person. Simply carry on quietly, stopping occasionally for very long searching looks at your subject, and they will soon wander away. Failure to do this may lead to inexpert and infuriating comments, a short history of their early talents, and a dramatised version of how great-uncle really should have been an artist but the family. . . . All of which may be interesting, but is guaranteed to spoil your painting.

Boost your morale by cutting a 'mount' which can be placed over your work: you will be surprised how much better it looks. A mount is merely a large piece of thick white card with a rectangle cut in it which is slightly smaller than your picture. It is very much like a large viewfinder, except that the bottom margin should be slightly wider than the other three. This frame around your work will make your assessment of its quality much more accurate.

If you decide to frame a picture, mount it first and then choose a quiet and neutral frame. The frame must never fight the painting by being over-dominant, as its purpose is to blend with the work and also to separate it from its surroundings.

The best subjects in summer are always to be found where there are thousands of flies, bluebottles and other insects. At least, such has been my experience. Keep a little bottle of insect repellent in your sketch-bag, and you can carry on painting in comfort whilst your friends are only to be seen through a cloud of buzzing and tickling marauders.

To Start You Painting

If your paints harden, they can be softened by one or two drops of glycerine. Should this not be available, place a damp folded rag across the paints over-night.

Should one of your favourite pieces of equipment have bolts and wing-nuts, it is a good plan to burr the end of the bolt with a hammer. This will damage the thread and prevent the wing-nut from spinning off and losing itself in the grass.

Always pack an extra cardigan or jersey. Sitting still can often be chilly, even on what appears to be quite a mild day, and nobody can work well if he is not relaxed and comfortable. A raincoat is essential too. The type that can be folded up very small is extremely useful. It is compact, will protect you from the odd shower, will act as a windcheater and, what is perhaps most important, can be used to protect the painting from rain spots.

It has often been said that a successful painting is one that you can live with. It is a good plan to prop up your mounted picture in some prominent place in the home. Look at it often. First thoughts are not always best; neither are the second. If after a fortnight a painting still pleases you, it is fairly safe to say your effort is successful.

View your work in a mirror! Often the sudden reversing of the composition will show up faults that had previously not been at all obvious.

Never despair at failures, for they are really stepping-stones. Artists have one thing in common with men who bet—they do not advertise their losses. All artists have their failures too, but without them success would never have been possible.

Remember that the road through the world of landscape-painting never ends, but the route is beautiful and refreshing. Keep your water clean, your colours fresh, your eyes wide open—and enjoy yourselves.